Second Edition

Greenman
and the Magic Forest

Starter
Forest Fun
Activity Book
Susannah Reed

Contents

Welcome to Forest School!

Find and colour the animals. Draw you.

3

Look. What's missing from the picture? Circle.

4

I look carefully.

NOW YOU! Sit and look outside.

Look around you. Find these things and circle.

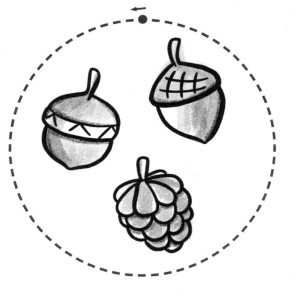

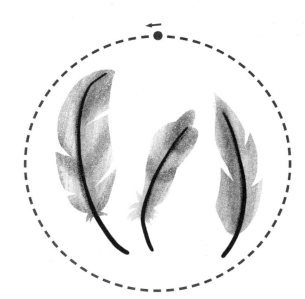

 I try hard.

 **Now you!** **Make a nature table.**

Trace. Draw what makes you happy.

 I feel happy.

 Do some yoga.

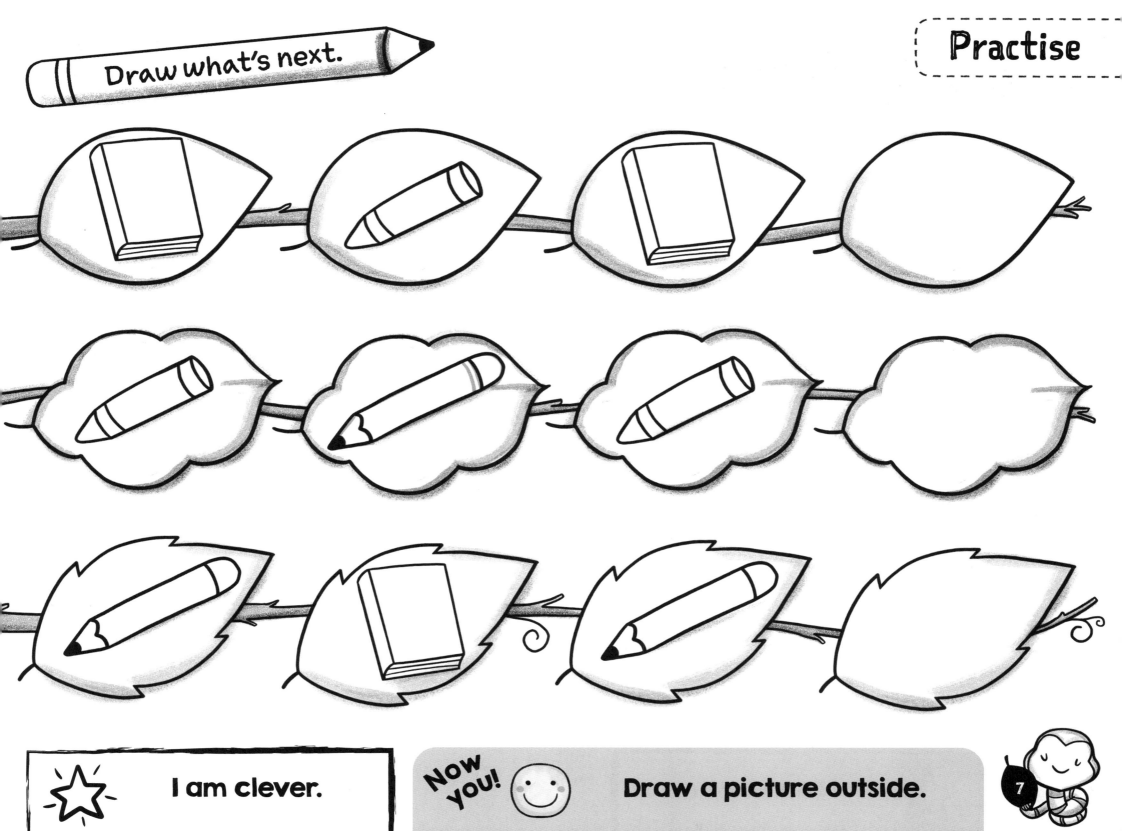

Draw what's next.

I am clever.

Now you! Draw a picture outside.

7

Trace and colour the circles.

 I can do it.

 **Look for circles in nature.**

Draw you and your friend.

I am a
good friend.

NOW
YOU!

Make a friendship tree.

Trace. Draw you.

I play outside.

Now you! Play outside.

Match the toys. Draw a teddy.

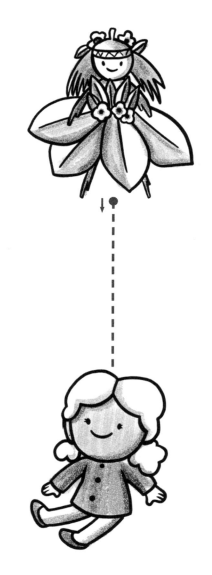

I use my imagination.

Now you! Make a forest toy.

Find the differences. Circle.

☆ I am clever.

 **Now you!** Have a race with toys.

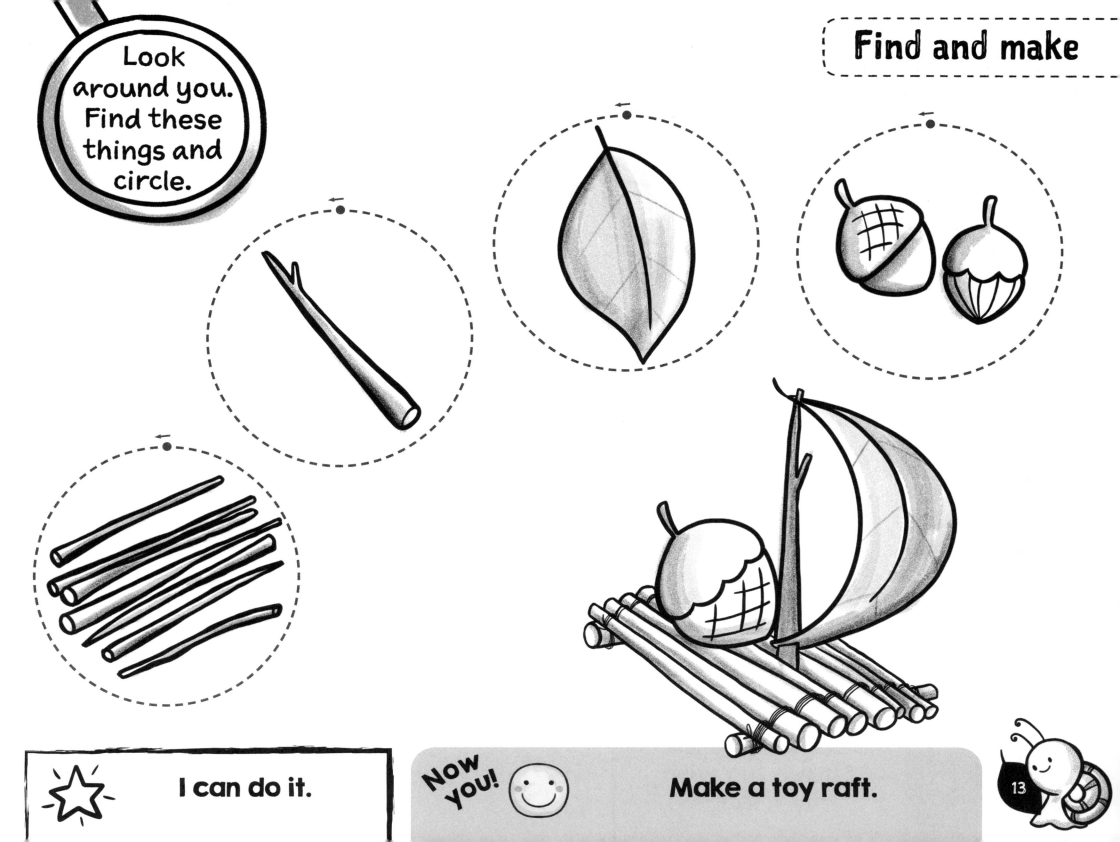

Look around you. Find these things and circle.

I can do it.

Now you! Make a toy raft.

13

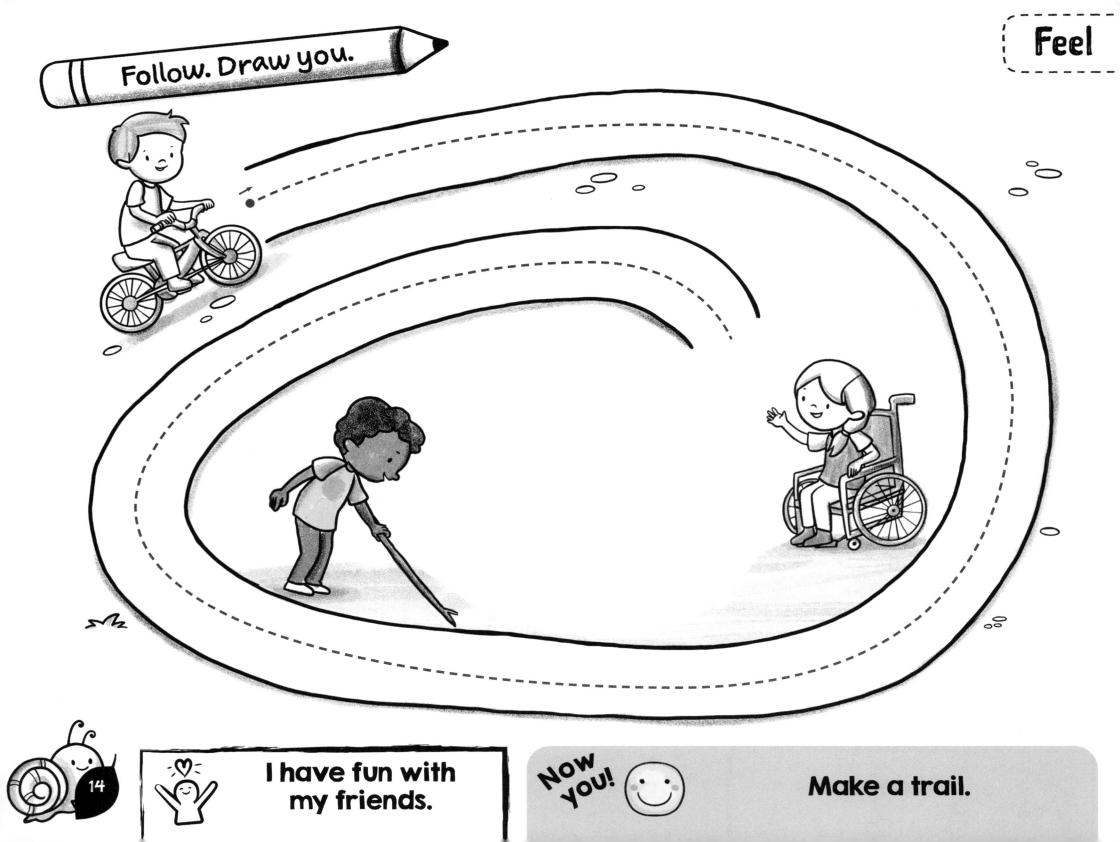

Follow. Draw you.

14

I have fun with my friends.

Now you!   Make a trail.

Find and colour the toys.

 **I take turns.**

Now you!  **Have a toy hunt.**

Look around you. Find these things and circle.

I am creative.

Now you!

Make a tree face.

Look. Circle the reflection.

I look carefully.

Now you! Look for your reflection.

Trace and colour the big things.

 I am interested in things.

 **Now you!** Look for small things.

Trace the face. Then draw you.

 I can do it.

Now you!  Draw pictures with a stick.

Think and draw what's in the cave.

20

I am kind to my friends.

Now you!

Do a flashlight walk.

Follow and colour to clean the pond.

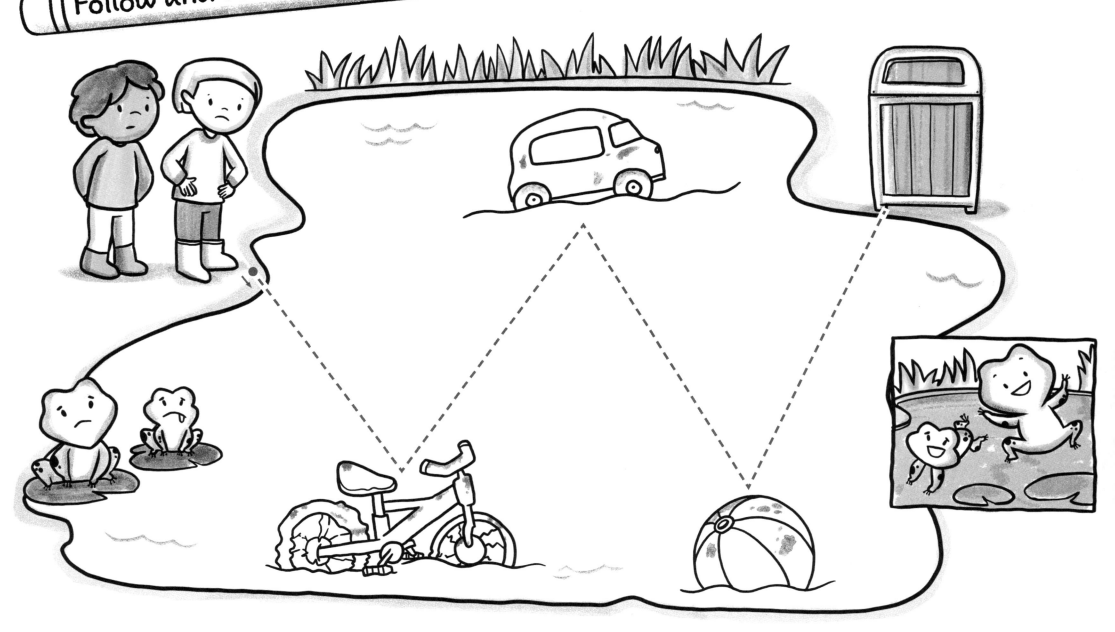

I care for the environment.

Now you! 😊   Tidy up toys.

Find the differences. Circle.

I look carefully.

NOW YOU! Watch animals outside.

Look around you. Find these things and circle.

I have good ideas.

Make a forest family.

Match. Colour the babies that are different.

 I am clever.

 Look for animal babies.

Help the baby find its family.

I care for animals.

Now You! Make an animal home.

Trace. Colour the number collages.

☆ I try hard.

Now YOU! Make a collage number.

Trace the triangles. Draw you.

 I feel good.

Now YOU! Do some yoga.

Match the animals to their homes.

 I look carefully.

 Now you!   Look for animal homes.

Look around you. Find these things and circle.

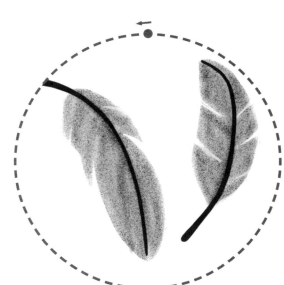

 I have good ideas.

 Now you! **Make forest wings.**

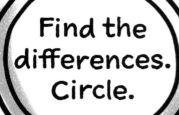

Find the differences. Circle.

I am clever.

Find animals.

Trace and colour the animals.

 I can do it.

Now you!  **Find symmetrical things.**

Draw the sun. Trace the cat.

I feel happy.

 Do some yoga.

Trace the bird. Draw a bird.

I care for animals.

Now you! Make a bird feeder.

Look. Think and draw things for the game.

 I use my senses.

 Play the smelling game.

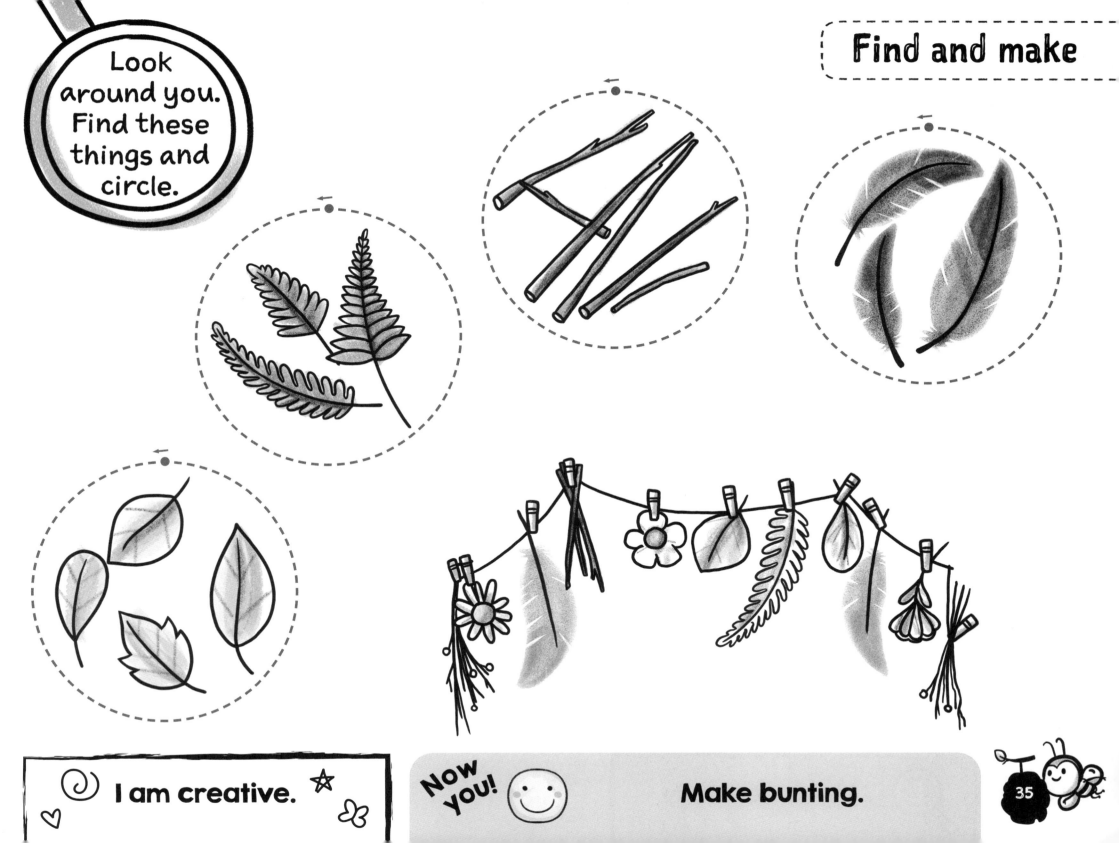

Look around you. Find these things and circle.

Find and make

I am creative.

Now you! Make bunting.

35

Find and colour the different food.

 36

I look carefully.

Now you!

Have a picnic.

Think and draw what they have made.

I say sorry.

 Now you!

Say sorry to a friend.

Circle the fruit. Draw it on the tree.

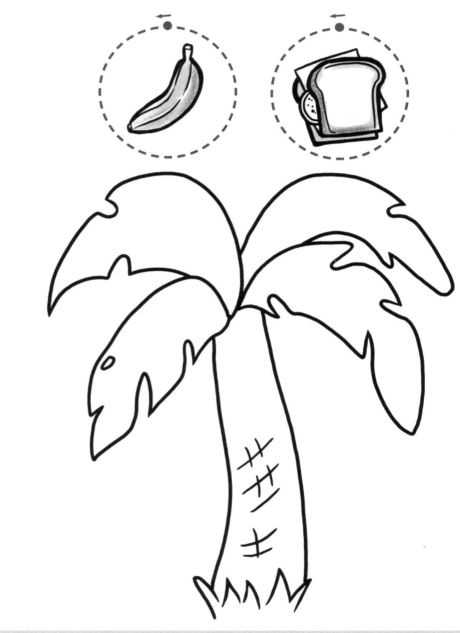

I am clever.

NOW YOU!

Plant an apple seed.

Find and circle the litter. Draw it in the bag.

I care for the environment.

NOW YOU! Pick up litter.

Shaftesbury Road, Cambridge CB2 8EA, United Kingdom

One Liberty Plaza, 20th Floor, New York, NY 10006, USA

477 Williamstown Road, Port Melbourne, VIC 3207, Australia

314–321, 3rd Floor, Plot 3, Splendor Forum, Jasola District Centre, New Delhi – 110025, India

103 Penang Road, #05–06/07, Visioncrest Commercial, Singapore 238467

José Abascal, 56–1º, 28003 Madrid, Spain

Cambridge University Press & Assessment is a department of the University of Cambridge.

We share the University's mission to contribute to society through the pursuit of education, learning and research at the highest international levels of excellence.

www.cambridge.org
Information on this title: www.cambridge.org/9781009219136

© Cambridge University Press & Assessment 2015, 2023

First published 2015
Second edition 2023

20 19 18 17 16 15 14 13 12 11 10 9 8 7 6 5 4 3 2

Printed in Spain by Coyve

Legal Deposit: M-25746-2022

A catalogue record for this publication is available from the British Library

ISBN 978-10-0921-913-6 Activity Book
ISBN 978-10-0921-908-2 Pupil's Book with Pupil's Digital Pack
ISBN 978-10-0921-914-3 Teacher's Book with Teacher's Digital Pack
ISBN 978-10-0921-944-0 Teacher's Book Castellano with Teacher's Digital Pack
ISBN 978-10-0921-947-1 Big Book
ISBN 978-10-0921-945-7 Flashcards
ISBN 978-10-0921-938-9 Classroom Presentation Software
ISBN 978-10-0921-912-9 Pupil's Online Resources
ISBN 978-10-0921-910-5 Home Practice E-book
ISBN 978-10-0921-948-8 Puppet

Cambridge University Press & Assessment has no responsibility for the persistence or accuracy of URLs for external or third-party Internet websites referred to in this publication and does not guarantee that any content on such websites is, or will remain, accurate or appropriate.

Acknowledgements

The authors and publishers acknowledge the following sources of copyright material and are grateful for the permissions granted. While every effort has been made, it has not always been possible to identify the sources of all the material used, or to trace all copyright holders. If any omissions are brought to our notice, we will be happy to include the appropriate acknowledgements on reprinting and in the next update to the digital edition, as applicable.

Illustration

Sheila Cabeza de Vaca

Typesetting

Aphik, S.A. de C.V.